An embrace in the dark-lit room

Carlotta Midolo

Presentation by *BookLeaf Publishing*

Web: www.bookleafpub.com

E-mail: info@bookleafpub.com

ISBN: 9789357446310

First edition 2022

DEDICATION

To my brother,

who protected me from the world,

before I even knew he was doing so.

PREFACE

"An embrace from the dark-lit room" is the eery comfort I find, in my connection with poetry. To me, this collection is nothing more than words, that entailed together, I hope will help me to illustrate my feelings and experiences. These poems were written in distinct moments, where I felt something so deeply I struggled to express it to anyone in simplistic terms, and a pen and paper, words on an ink where my only dear friend. I hope everyone who reads makes each piece their own. I hope you find something inside this that's personal to you. I hope that in the midst of the disarray and mayhem, you discover the solace, alleviation and hope which writing these very poems filled me with.

Achingly alone yet infinitely together

All I knew is you made me want to inhale the
moon,
until its splendour lights up my ribcage,
to keep our secrets within the folds of my
blanket
to hold them,
as we somehow both secretly know,
there's no stopping this fast and far fall into
madness.

How could one star shine so bright?
How could you never burn out?
For as improbable of a concept as love is
to our strange organs,
I struggle and strain to explain the awe of you,
for you are like nothing I have ever seen.

I like to think you're an embrace from tomorrow
an immeasurable love like no other,
and as I listen to your melodies,
I realise more and more
that to live a life without you,
would be to live no life at all.

My mother

Mesmerize the tragedies and tell me nothing is
real
but the sand under our feet,
the overpowering scent of the oranges from
grandmother's cake,
the warmth from your arms.
You made sacrifices so I'd never have to,
I observed your every move, your every step,
every sound, every utterance I could register
because the first answer that came to mind
whenever someone asked
"What do you wanna be when you grow up?
was you.

But I quickly learnt that you are every shade of
happiness and strength
I can't even begin to comprehend,
every ray of streetlight that cuts through the
blinds in my room
the air filling my lungs,
giving me the capability to breathe,
to exist
to live and feel alive.

And so, knowing I'd only fail,
I stopped wanting to be you,
because I understood the galaxies didn't take
time for granted when you were sculpted,
carefully planned and designed until you could
hold your own hand and flourish.
And even in the bars of a lunar prison,
you always brightened my dreams back up,
and still now,
there's no place like my mother's light beams
and tender arms.

I'm sorry. Is my existence disturbing you?

How unladylike of me to wear skirts and
strapless tops during summer,
when hair's clearly visible on my legs and
underarms,
what a scandal to leave the house in such a
manner.
How offensive of me to converse about my
period,
or ask questions on the biology of my most
intimate body parts.
Oh gosh,
is it also unfeminine of me to ask my older
brother to buy pads on my behalf?
Or for my friends to succeed in your
male-dominated fields?
Should we apologise now for being talented in
sports?
or maybe it's best to save that for later,
over the homecooked meal, I will never prepare
for you.

But at least YOU don't have to lower your voice.

How valiant of you to speak of what you did
when I shook my head repeatedly,
when I couldn't find a voice to scream that I
didn't want to be touched,
to steal what little power I had,
and leave me terrified of my own voice.

Speechless for you.

I'd be lying if I said
you render me speechless,
the truth is -
you make my tongue so weak,
it forgets what language to speak in,
and my lips so frail,
they lose all ability
yet not that to merely curl into a smile

but I know that's my heart's
command,
taking control of my body,
to respond to you.

Your final theft

When we stopped, everything shifted
everything around me was the same,
just with a lack of you.

You were never a curse,
and the dark-filled silence held my tears in its
hands for months,
but it's only when another human stopped
existing as my reason for
being and living,
that I realised the only permanent antidote I
needed
was in a place I'd least expect to find it.
I stopped creating prisons and phrases to hide
behind,
I stopped looking outwards for love,
and found I am my own soulmate.
And I saw the world was never stolen from me,
The ability to perceive its beauty was simply lost
within me.

You can't make a home out of beings
that aren't you.

What have I become?

Just that enormous scorching rage
towards yourself
me
myself
I don't want to be me anymore
I don't want to be what I am,
what I've become
because I know it's all my fault
but I don't want to accept that.
It's better to blame it on some imaginary thing,
like that I'm not truly within my body,
like my brain isn't mine to be in control of, or
that my soul is disconnected from my body.
I want to take responsibility for what I've done
but that would mean I would have to open a
window,
turn my face towards what I've been turning
away from my whole life
push apart the blinds in one swift motion,
and let in the light
to show what I've done
and who I've become
and, am I ready to face myself?

Woman and war

Medusa slept,
yet the snakes in her hair never did.
Condemned to be monstrous,
deemed repulsively grotesque for centuries to
come,
she spent the abyss unable to adore another's
eyes again.
Previously graceful strands of identity and
being,
converted unjustly by another
into a weapon,
war and woman,
unbearable, blinding and petrifying-
so powerful it confined both those unlucky
enough to spare a glance,
and her very entity,
eternally imprisoned away from nature's solace.
War within a woman,
something not everyone is capable to
comprehend,
something not everyone knows how to love.

Dreaming of our legacy

Hand in hand,
we're gazing at everything we've created
our little world,
a legacy.
"What will you leave behind?" they'd ask us,
I am yet to understand what they expected -
maybe a fortune,
maybe kids,
maybe our very downfall.
Does it truly hold any significance?
Isn't the solar eclipse of our love,
intertwined in these very lines,
enough?

Hand in hand,
We're gazing at everything we've created,
collapse and crumble,
enthusiasm and affection,
uncontrollable heartbeats and bitten smiles,
homage and tears.
That's what we'll live behind:
fireflies that hold our very history,

a warning of flashing locked memories;
the very promise that there's more to life than
just living,
that somewhere out there lies our dream of
utopia.

If you forget our promises, look to the clouds.

You could make my bruises fade tender,
cover the world's mistakes in your ichor dusk,
but what I truly choose to see is you,
your fleeting warmth hold hands with my heart,
and it's almost like my wounds aren't hurting
anymore,
they feel like a re-do button,
a new day,
a chance to start over,
a beginning!

And, I look across the road and imagine our
shapes and shadows in each other's companies,
and in between whispers and feeling touched by
the stars,
I like to think our i love you's,
travel safe and lock themselves
within gaps of air in the sky.

Harmful to me.
Harmful to you.

My gaze loses itself and our memories appear in
my view,
I see that I don't own them anymore,
in the small corner of our universe,
and yet it felt grander when it was you and me -
when these memories were mine,
ours.

We began talking to each other,
talking at each other, rather-
and we were only saying the words we wanted
to hear back.
We were in this echo filled broken room,
yet we still thought that our voices would carry,
in fact, I think they did,
they travelled quite far,
they touched the cool tides below and met in the
middle,
and in that moment,
they collided and destroyed each other.
Destroy each other until we couldn't distinguish
the darkness from our shadows?

Isn't that what we were really trying to do
anyway?

And so, our voices travelled,
over and over,
and we continued to lose communication,
until we lost everything altogether.

Humanity

I cross my legs whilst on the carpet
of my childhood bedroom,
as the last notes ring out
and my deepest despairs seem to rejoice.

Today, it feels like all I have left is my humanity
and I always come back to this in my mind,
and in a weak endeavour to feel like totality
doesn't own me,
I wonder if once again I'll confuse obscurity
with wonderment.

I can nearly hear the final act,
the final quivering from the strings,
the lowest timbre of all should be any second
now,
and as the solemn echoes fill with what seems to
be
a pure, truly marvellous life in disguise
the orchestra plays out the final semibreve,
and even now,
despite the dread of the stinging vibrations,
I long to hear more.

Shot through the art

My anger is boiling
everyone's holding the same gun
infiltrated with venom but the smoke signals its
empty
the bullets must've been fired already
how could I have missed it
how could I have confused the trigger for a
paintbrush
consumed by the splatter
in awe of the red
I thought I saw the shade of adoration,
tenderness, intimacy
your love,
all for me
instead it was all over me,
blood,
and all over your hands
with the gun still wrapped around your fingers.

I hope you find pride in your work,
I hope the canvas is all you wanted it to be.
How talented are you?
The precision in the brushstrokes full of
ammunition
you shot the artwork

testing my sanity
I don't know what's worse
what you did or that I allowed you to.
You didn't even disguise it as a painting,
I put up my own exhibition of your oeuvre
an immersive - my favourite kind
the only one I truly manage to get lost into.

You didn't do this.
I did.
The blood is on my hands.
you simply held the gun right to my forehead
as our eyes met
and i fell in love with yours
full of a need for betrayal I still can't grasp.

Incomplete.

Where would this thought even go
what smudge on the wall will the light shed on
maybe this is my very own red-room,
my darkroom,
a photo I'll never develop,
am I making more excuses?
am I losing it?
is it all pointless?
Hanging a half-finished imagine across a
singular washing line.

Incomplete
Is that what this is?
Is that what I am'?
Maybe it's best to be honest,
to just admit we're not safe here,
maybe the worst of the danger is in pretending
we are.
These words are nothing more than ink stains on
my hands
nothing that would make sense to someone that's
not me,
maybe there's a beauty in the fact that right now
I'm incomplete.

Absolution

Your thoughts take on flesh,
and become an ambush,
a singular, simplistic plan to destroy,
consuming every red flicker,
a bitter blade piercing the lungs,
a contemplation of the philosophy of existing
and yet lacking the ability to live.

And so we're forced to drag our bodies forward,
grinning at life through an empty joy
aimlessly choosing a path each day.
When will I wake up and see that
writing to the point of suffocation
isn't liberating?
When will we wake up and see
acceptance isn't life's greatest beauty?
Forgiving oneself is.

Sombre epitome

I find that the night is very much alive
we're born beside it
we exhale the fumes of its silence
we let its infinitely receding distance nurture us,
whilst the stars gleam through our bedroom
windows,

but if we cross the line of the night,
I'm dangerously secure that we'll never be able
to turn back.

The threat lies in how we let it consume us,
the stillness we detest cradles our thoughts
the noise we hate it's
useless, aimless, uninhabited,
but we stay awake, silent and repeat
again
and words overlap in the shadows,
notions reach dusk

but as I continue rambling,
I see light outside too
the moonlight, the stars, the fluorescent street
lights,

and I remember our bodies, alive, living, laying
right there
I remember our chests rising and dropping,
in the middle ground between light and shadow
and suddenly I'm out of the sombre epitome that
is my head,
and suddenly,
that noise we hate it's
essential, purposeful,
it's home

For my brother

For as long as I can remember, my brother
safe-guarded me.
I didn't always understand this,
but every bike ride and tickling hysteria,
every ball-catching game played far away in a
deeper end of the sea,
every rock ballad implanted into my brain,
every plastic plate in the drumkit of our
no-hit-wonder band,
every time he scooted over and let me stay with
him,
without uttering a word during midnight
nightmares,
was always his way of easing the storm,
of providing me with shelter.

To this day, I'm not sure how to express my
gratitude,
but all I know was when terror inaudibly
slithered in from the unfixable crack of my
bedroom window,
and the rhythmic rate of everything around me
rises to be uncontrollable,
my brother took moments in time and altered my
memory of them,

he is the reason I smile when I look back at
certain events.

He sat with me in a terrible place,
and convinced me we were always safe.

Traces of a juvenile

My mother called me a sponge today,
soaking in all,
even that which isn't mine to hold,
and it made me think of someone I knew.

Oblivious on how we lost touch,
I searched for you
within the 206 bones,
78 organs
and over 7 trillion nerves,
you still unclenched your little fingers
and faded away from my grasp,
and I like to imagine
you're somewhere still running around the soft
velvet of our white curtain,
still close to home.

I hope one day she'll trust me again,
I hope she'll learn all men don't resemble him.
I hope she's running so fast from whoever is
chasing her up the stairs,
and learns that sleeping with the light on doesn't
mean she's weak.
I hope you're not the reason she never writes
again,

I hope she becomes the warrior we were
promised but couldn't be.

A note to you,
may you memorise a thousand gazes,
before seeing the brightest gleam stems from
your very own eyes.
You will plant a thousand seeds,
before learning the most beautiful flowers only
grow
when you find love for the very same hands
which nurtured the roots.

A man looking at the world through a keyhole.

The drumming footsteps against your
windowsill are all your crimes.

Each drop is every single act you hold yourself
accountable for,
every single transgression,
every fault, every offence you can't forgive
yourself for committing,
every baggage of wrongdoing and monstrosity
you'll always force yourself to carry on your
back,
and as the puddles on the cement thrive and
bloom,
what happens to the flower within you?

As the echoes of laughing voices across the
street run outside,
the sky clears up,
and for a second, that's all there is,
a sharp intake of breath,

the sound of a heart monitor beeping,
voices of a muffled crowd,
a feeling of lightheadedness.
And yet, you still can't seem to have learnt,
you don't appear to see the refraction of light
after a storm,
the absence of anything,
the existence of everything.

You're stuck in the prison of the rain,
and self condemnation will corrupt all that's left
in you,
and you'll fail once again to take a glimpse at the
gathering of colours in the clouds,
the canvas of the sky,
all because you couldn't forgive your bruises,
you let the rain clutch onto you and it was too
late to save you,
you swam down too deep.

Are you here, friend?

I am not writing poetry, dear.
I am showing you frozen memories embedded in
my mind,
moments in time I like to think atoms collide
an electron hitting a photon of light
a head gasping for air, emerging out of the water
a piano piece played with simple, majestic finger
movements
I am sharing the depths of my heart with you.

I am not writing poetry, friend.
I'm holding a mirror,
I've set up a camera on a 21 second self-timer,
and I think you're trying to find yourself in the
frame,
I'm inexplicably curious to see
if you can find your own reflection in these very
words and concepts.
You keep turning the page,
You read and explore,
and still I wonder,
Can you see yourself?

You're the real poem.
I am merely a stranger writing down the
fragments of it all.

Tear after tear

It's something so inconceivably grey that it falls
into line without murmur
that initial feeling of hollowness,
where the world could end
and you could just lay there,
with the lights turned off,
no energy, not even for the tears.

And then all at once,
the air in my chest turns into a thin space,
the tears begin falling,
poison slowly taking its course within your
veins,
my ragged organs are drenched of all life,
the tears keep falling,
and the silence morphs into islands of violence
the tears keep falling,
and in this field of screaming roses,
the danger keeps clinging.

Only when you're able to finally match your
gaze with the darkness,
Will you be able to win and be free?
The tears finally stop.
This is it.

You + atoms + nature = imminent beauty.

You are carved out of everything you find
beautiful in the world.
Your body is a delicately manufactured machine
of molecules, atoms, hydrogen,
everything stars hanging upon the sky contain
too
the sun's harmonious morning spectacle,
the ocean's joyful screams in the crashing waves.

The world is made out of you,
and tonight, on the grand scheme of the
universe,
it is indeed everything.
You are all the parts of the most powerful storm,
thunder, lightening, rain, wind,
and if the universe is a remarkably extraordinary
place,
surely, there can be no denying you are as
beautiful as everything in it.